Rainy Day:
Wondering

Poems for a Rainy Day

Gary W. Burns

Turning Corner Books ™

WWW.TURNINGCORNERBOOKS.COM

Copyright © 2010 by Vista View Publishing
PO Box121, Haymarket, VA 20168

All rights reserved under International
And Pan-American Copyright Conventions.
Published in the United States by Turning Corner Books.

Library of Congress Control Number: 2010927199
ISBN: 978-0-9845342-5-8

Third Printing, May 2018

Manufactured in the United States
Designed by the author; artwork by the author.

Other Books of Poetry
by Gary W. Burns

Bridges: To There
      (Poems for the Mind, Body & Spirit)

Clouds: On the Wind
      (Poems for the Soul – A Meditation)

Earth Tones: A Journey
      (Poetry for the Journey)

Garden Walks: Hand In Hand
      (Poems To Relax By)

Moments: This to the Next
      (Poetry - Now and Eternity)

Poems of Love: A Selection

To You With Love: Selected Poems

Twilight: Awaking the Stars
      (Poems of the Night's Light)

To My Children
Miracles

CONTENTS

i

◆ Storms and Things

◆ Raindrops and Windows

♦ Gifts of the Rain

Gray Day Wondering

Rainy Day Song

Joyous voices
Resound
As a pitter-patter
And a pitter-patter
Upon the window
Is found.

How wonderful
The sound
Of rain
Coming down.

Woven

With the wind
To my back
Moving me quickly

And you

Out there who
I'm looking for
And who's

Looking for me
Too

Moving
As well so quickly;

We'll meet
By design.

Relax

I know
Sometimes
Slowing down
Is hard to do

I invite you,

Relaxingly

Relax

Clarinet

Loving Eyes

1

We could wrap our arms
Around one another,
Move,
Breath to breath,
Sway,
Touch to touch,
And know
The heat
Of love.

2

But, it's
The wonder
Of the love
That I see
In your loving eyes
That I want wed
To the vastness of me.

3

Wanting it so, please
Allow me
To be
The love I see
In your
        loving eyes.

In Rainy Day: Wondering

Dancing

Light,
Dancing
With its partner,

Whirls us

In steps
Eternal.

Piano

Motion

Towards,
Traversing,
Away;

Our fate

Both
Night and day.

Gray Day
Wondering

1

The misty rain
Grays the day
And blurs
The cityscape view.

2

But, I see you
Your sun dress
Waving in the wind
And a sky blue
Surrounding
A noonday sun.

The one
We walked beneath
While holding hands
As we strolled the beach.

Talking.

3

Tomorrow,
Being so far out of sight
Made everything we did
Though that day and night
Alright.

4

How wonderful
The wandering mind
On rainy days,
Opening vistas wide
Of memories deep.

I hope you're well
And wish you love.

Full Orchestra

Smiling

I'm not going to say,
Smile for the world
When you're blue

Or pretend happy
When you're not.

But, life
Has taught

Me this,

Be your day sunny
Or blue
Smile for you.

The Light
Of Love

Be true to you,
The light of love.

Large Steps

1

There are those
Who can't see the forest
For the trees.

And again,

Those
Who can't see the trees
For the leaves.

And those
Who can't see the flowers
For the weeds.

2

And of course
There are those
Who
Can't take the large step
For the fall.

3

But, perhaps,
Just perhaps,
There's no size
At all
And the large
Is the same
As the small
After all.

Beyond Circles

At the end of one
Is the beginning
Of the other one

So "one"
Never ends

Within You

A smile, a frown,

Furrowed brow,
Dimpled cheeks,

Baby's tears,
Wrinkles
From the years:

I see forever
Within you,
And you, and you.

No other place
Will do.

Write Me

1

Where lies
The wellspring
Of Life . . . ?

In, out
All about

Up, down,
Around

An appearance,
An Illusion

2

Open to view
Hidden from sight

In love, in might

A secret, a truth

Less,
More . . . ?

Where lies
The wellspring
Of Life . . . ?

3

Write me.

Unknown

The pond
Was frozen over.

I saw the geese
There today,
A flock
Atop the ice.

To me
It didn't seem
Cold to them, just,
Part of it all;
Unknown.

Soon

Translucent raindrops
Wait
Patiently
On the blue iris.

The sun is out
And soon
Sunrays will consume
The waiting droplets.

Love,
Translucent,
Waits patiently.

The sun is out,
Love;
Soon.

Each Day Dear

1

How is it possible
I feel the gray
Of day,

The why I know.

For you
Dearest sunshine
Once shining
Here in every part
Of this heart
Did
In sunray play
But now,
You've gone away.

2

You've gone
With her
Elsewhere
And there
Shine
As you did
When you were mine.

But O not to worry,
For certainly,
Sunrays, like days,
Have ways
Of coming back.

So,
No frowns here
Only eyes shining clear
For I know how dear

Each day be.

Storms
and Things

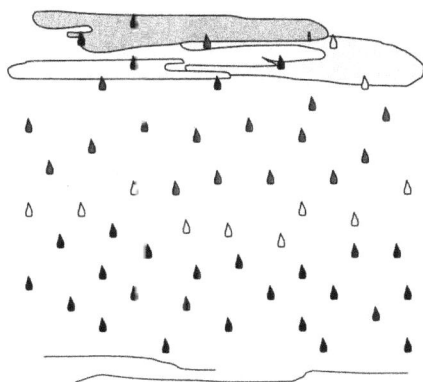

Rain
Drumming

Rain
Drumming
Upon tree tops

Clouds
Foreboding

Stormy winds
Kowtowing
Leaves and limbs

Then lightning
Then thunder -

Persevere

Out of the Rain

Come in
Out of the rain.

The lightning strike's
Too bright
For sight,
The pelting rain
Too much of a sting,
The cold wind
Too blustery.

The door's open.

Come in
Out of the rain.
Into the arms
            of love.

Beginnings

Love starts
In the heart.

Begin.

You
And I

No "I"
Is singular;
For what be "I"
Without
    "You".

Sooner or Later

There's no hiding

From raindrops

Eventually
We get wet

It's best
To keep walking

Sooner or later

The sun comes out

Mile After Mile

1

Many miles
Have gone by;
The smiles along the way
Were comforting.

2

Some smiles
Said hello,
Some said,
Let's get to know
One another,
Others
Were simply smiles
Passing by;

Mile after mile,
Sunrise after sunrise,
Night after night.

3

Thinking
There has to be
A meaning to it all
We have to make it
Mean something;
Or so we believe.

4

What offers more,
Searching
For some meaning
Or Loving
And knowing
Love means everything

Mile after mile,
Sunrise after sunrise
And night after night.

Growing

Sometimes,
People
Grow together.
Sometimes,
People
Grow apart.

But,
It's all
In the growing;
Keep growing
In mind,
Spirit,
And heart.

Harmony

Loves'
Grace;
Rainbows'
Light.

In Rainy Day: Wondering

Your Smile

Smiles
Are invitations

So what about
    the smiles
You gave away
    today

And those
    of yesterday

And those
    of tomorrow

    and tomorrow

    and tomorrow

The Key

I wonder,
And that,
Has given me
The key
To me.

Your love,
My heart beat.

———————————————

One day
My heart will stop

And then . . .

———————————————

Whispers
Embrace

People

Some people
Can't sleep.

Some people
Never want to wakeup.

Someone New

1

Some leaves
            will
Ride the breeze
Across the pond
And never get wet
            some won't.

2

I left behind
            memories
And because
            I did
Things
      are forgotten.

3

It's best that way
        anyway
For what good
        would it do
For me
To remember
Things about you

When I'm looking
    for someone new.

Chasing
Rainbows

I know
I chase rainbows
My friend.

You see,
After the twist
And turns of storms
Rainbows
Are a welcome sight;

Soft to the eye
And gentle
To the emotions.

Chasing rainbows
Is okay
With me.

Tranquility

Silence
And me.

In Rainy Day: Wondering

Raindrops
and Windows

The Wonder
Of Love

You caught
My attention

As you rustled
Autumn leaves,

Spurred
Blue-green seas,

And touched
My face

As I turned
Toward you
Not yet knowing

You'd comfort me
Eternally

Love

Life

In everything
We do

You give to me
I give to you.

What A Wonderful While

There was a time
For a while
When
Time didn't matter

And our knowing
Was filled with

Smiles

What a wonderful while

Raining Down

Curious clouds coming;
Care approaching.

Edges disappear,
The rain is here.

The nurture
Of nature;
Giving.

Love's
Raining down.

Lines

Life should be full.
One should be round.

No lines
To where I'm bound.

Oh Hello

There are
The last days of things,
The goodbyes,
And the going away.

But me,
I prefer to dwell in
Hello.

For,
For all I know,
Every end
Begins again.

Yours,
Eternally

Opus

Silence
Silently
Serenading

The Ring

1

The ring of seasons
Parading . . .

2

Here
In the deep woods
Quietly

It's raining down
Autumn leaves
From colorful trees

And things
Are preparing
For what winter brings.

3

O ring
You wellspring.

Is there
Something new
In what's old,
Something old
In what's new

Or
Are they one
In two . . .

Too Far

Let's not think
Too far ahead

Nor think
Too far behind,

As a matter of fact
Thinking "now"
Is just fine.

Secrets

The brook runs
From where . . .

There's no telling.

The Kiss
Missed

1

How could we
Have said
   good-bye
And not have
   touched lips
Held
One another's
   hand
And pressed
     softly
   against
One another.

2

It's the kissed
 never kissed
That lingers
 and is missed,

And is missed,

 and missed,

 and missed,
 and missed.

Cello

What Greater Gift

1

Perhaps,
I shouldn't speak
Of love.

That light
That's too bright
To see.

That darkness
That holds each of us
Intimately.

2

But,
My heart beats
Because of loves'
Resound.

And in its glory
I'm found.

3

Perhaps,
I shouldn't speak
Of love.

But,
What greater gift
Is there to speak of
Than love.

Seeing
Love

The lens
Of the eye
Is small

But its depth
Goes
Forever

Seeing
Love

Gifts
of the Rain

Gift Giver

O joyous rain
Falling with love
Setting anew
And rekindling
Too.

Marvel

I saw beauty fleeting;
What was I to do.

Wrapped
In the arms of awe
And held so tightly

I could not pursue.

Moonbeams

Morning
Came home dry
Under nights
Starry umbrella.

But us,
We two
Get wet

As moonbeams
Rained down.

Musing

1

The whispering wind
Gently spoke
And awoke
The dreamy folk
Who

Looking round
Found

2

Skies
To please the eyes,

Meadows
Stretching lazily,

Seas
Tossing,

And beauty
Aplenty

So
You'er
A Dreamer

So
You're a rainy day
Dreamer,

I am too;

Dreaming
of you.

Things I Do

Thank
You;
For-giving-me
The things
            I do.

Wait

Wait,
Don't go
Too far
Without me:
   Love.

Dew Drops

Can you
Listen to the quiet

Can you
Hear the silence

Then

You know
Love

The Smell of the Rain

The smell of the rain
Upon the streets
Or upon autumn leaves,
In the mountain dale,
Or along the seashore

Brings to me

Peace.

The Beauty

The beauty
Of wonder
Wraps
About me
The mantle
Of life.

Now
That It's Raining

1

I felt
A drop or two
Of rain.

What do you
Want to do?

We could hide away
Or
Celebrate the rain.

2

I could hold you
And you
Would know my arms
And they
Would reveal my heart.

What do you want to do
Now

That it's raining

Violin

Utah Buttes

1

I saw the rains coming
Over the Utah buttes;

You can't stop the rains
From coming.

2

I've heard it said heartaches
Make you wiser for the knowing.

I think you can be wise
Without them.

But, nonetheless,
You can't stop the rains
Or the heartaches
From coming.

2

The buttes didn't much care
About the rains, emotionless
Monoliths.

I guess I'd rather feel
Than be a grand monolith
In the rain.

We can't stop the rains
Or the heartaches
From coming.

Love Me

Words
Are illusive

Touch

Softly

Love me

Said Love

And who will love this child

I will

Said love

As the rains came down

THROUGH THE RAIN . . .

About the Author

Inspired by nature and the beauty around him Gary W. Burns started writing poetry at a young age. Early on Gary was able to express his thoughts, ideas and emotions through the vivid imagery of his verse. His poetry has been published in various literary arts journals, anthologies and magazines. He is the author of 10 books of poetry. Through his poems Gary shares his reflections on the many facets of life and on the beauty of nature. The expressiveness of his poetry has been enriched by his wide reading in philosophy and psychology. He has traveled throughout the world and has lived in numerous countries, to include, Italy, Korea, Saudi Arabia and Canada. He has also lived in Hawaii and several other states. Currently, Gary makes his home in Northern Virginia near the foothills of the Blue Ridge Mountains.

ENJOY THESE OTHER BOOKS OF POETRY BY GARY W. BURNS

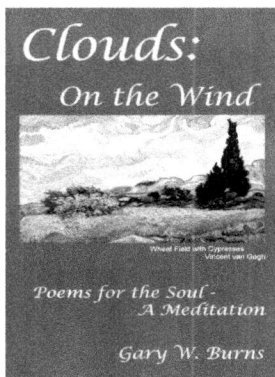

Clouds: On the Wind
(Poems for the Soul - A Meditation)
ISBN: 978-0-9845342-0-2 (Paperback)
ISBN: 978-0-9845342-1-0 (Hardcover)
ISBN: 978-0-986090-3-5 (E-Book)

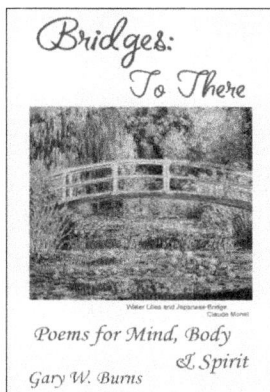

Bridges: To There
(Poems for the Mind, Body & Spirit)
ISBN: 978-0-9827805-6-5 (Paperback)
ISBN: 978-0-9827805-7-2 (Hardcover)
ISBN: 978-0-9860900-4-2 (E-Book)

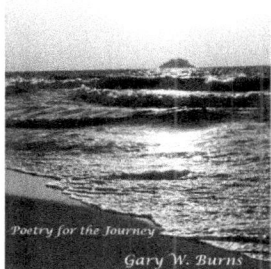

Earth Tones: A Journey
(Poetry for the Journey)
ISBN: 978-0-9845342-6-5 (Paperback)
ISBN: 978-0-9845342-9-6 (Hardcover)
ISBN: 978-0-9860900-8-0 (E-Book)

To You With Love: Selected Poems
ISBN: 978-0-9845342-6-5 (Paperback)
ISBN: 978-0-9827805-3-4 (Hardcover)
ISBN: 978-0-9860900-2-8 (E-Book)

Garden Walks: Hand In Hand
(Poems To Relax By)
ISBN: 978-0-9845342-3-4 (Paperback)
ISBN: 978-0-9827805-0-3 (Hardcover)
ISBN: 978-0-9860900-1-1 (E-Book)

Poems of Love: A Selection
ISBN: 978-0-9845342-8-9 (Paperback)
ISBN: 978-0-9827805-5-8 (Hardcover)
ISBN: 978-0-9860900-5-9 (E-Book)

Available at WWW.TURNINGCORNERBOOKS.COM and where books are sold.

www.ingramcontent.com/pod-product-compliance
Lightning Source LLC
Chambersburg PA
CBHW072151020426
42334CB00018B/1955